YOUR KNOWLEDGE HAS VALUE

- We will publish your bachelor's and
  master's thesis, essays and papers

- Your own eBook and book -
  sold worldwide in all relevant shops

- Earn money with each sale

Upload your text at www.GRIN.com
and publish for free

Ryan Edwards

The controversy surrounding 'Queer as Folk'

Banality of current TV or society's persistent homophobia?

GRIN Verlag

Bibliografische Information der Deutschen Nationalbibliothek:

Die Deutsche Bibliothek verzeichnet diese Publikation in der Deutschen National-
bibliografie; detaillierte bibliografische Daten sind im Internet über http://dnb.d-
nb.de/ abrufbar.

Imprint:

Copyright © 2001 GRIN Verlag GmbH
Druck und Bindung: Books on Demand GmbH, Norderstedt Germany
ISBN: 978-3-656-74660-7

This book at GRIN:

http://www.grin.com/en/e-book/280268/the-controversy-surrounding-queer-as-folk

GRIN - Your knowledge has value

Der GRIN Verlag publiziert seit 1998 wissenschaftliche Arbeiten von Studenten, Hochschullehrern und anderen Akademikern als eBook und gedrucktes Buch. Die Verlagswebsite www.grin.com ist die ideale Plattform zur Veröffentlichung von Hausarbeiten, Abschlussarbeiten, wissenschaftlichen Aufsätzen, Dissertationen und Fachbüchern.

Visit us on the internet:

http://www.grin.com/

http://www.facebook.com/grincom

http://www.twitter.com/grin_com

Does the controversy surrounding the series 'Queer as Folk' reveal more the banality of current TV or society's persistent homophobia?

Introduction

There have been times in television history where certain programmes have tackled society's taboos in a particularly vivid way by coming to fruition at sometimes sensitive times. For example the controversial topic of the sixties was of immigration and the media's double edged ability both inflamed public opinion through newsprint and reflected their concerns through controversial comedy sitcoms such as 'Love Thy Neighbour' and 'Bless This House' which both dealt with the then taboo of race. As within any cultures what is deemed acceptable and unacceptable changes over time and so it could be said that Queer as Folk (QAF) is a nineties' equivalent of such shows.

Homosexuality is arguably one of the last remaining taboos in many cultures and one that dominates the topic of social change, particularly in the West. This notion of taboo was blatantly challenged when the first episode involved consensual gay sex between an adult and a 15-year-old. Much has been said on this topic in recent years as society's views have gradually liberalised, as the traditional societal unit, marriage, has fallen into terminal decline. In this context the new Labour government has, since taking office in 1997 attempted to introduce several equality laws, most significantly equalising the age of consent and the repeal of section 28[1] that disallows the 'promotion' of homosexuality in schools. The political impact of this show is acutely measured in Peter Billingham's *Sensing the City through Television* where he refers to a letter from the National Viewer's and Listener's Association[2] to the Independent Television Commission (ITC) on the 24th Feb 1999:

---

[1] This was successful in the Scottish assembly though was repeatedly frustrated in Westminster by a House of Lords conservative revolt led by Baroness young, See www.stonewall.org.uk
[2] Founded by Mary Whitehouse – the paradigm of meridian reactionary values

This programme is calculated to influence public opinion at a time when the age of homosexual consent is being debated in Parliament [Billingham 2000:121]

In a similar vein to the controversial shows of the sixties, the newspapers have had a feeding frenzy stoking public opinion and yet the other side of the media, TV has sought to tackle issues in a different way through an unexpectedly acclaimed drama series and its sequel. Such a show therefore must contain substantial communication techniques and so I felt aside from personal interest it would prove a valid subject to research into. Within the media, much is made of controversy; indeed it could be considered a vital element of, for example, the music industry.

Therefore I decided to frame my research around the reasons Queer as Folk caused such controversy, identifying two potential strands. Firstly whether the construction and content of the show was radically different from its peers in an era when TV is increasingly referred to as banal and 'dumbed down'. Secondly to attempt to gauge whether our society has indeed liberalised its attitudes to homosexuality and the subsequent affect such media texts have. Regarding the actual construction of the research question, I am making the assumption that the level of controversy was unusually high and so builds revelations above the normal controversy that some shows intentionally promote just to increase ratings.

Background

My aims for this research are numerous. Firstly I wanted to subject aspects of the show to a communication studies analysis which I hope would further my understanding and appreciation of the show while revealing interesting results. Widening the scope onto the media industry and how such a show is communicated and its effects. Also I wanted to scratch beneath the surface of common assumptions; for example whether the gay population is as homogenous as the press would have you believe. To this end I highlighted two methods of inquiry that would prove most fruitful within the limitations of this research. Firstly the methods of surveys and sampling in order to ascertain opinion on my two main research strands and to qualify my theories, taking into careful account a review of what literature there has been around the series. Secondly the method of selective content and textual analysis as research into the cultural level of controversy and communication techniques used. I will be discussing epistemological issues in so far as I will be deconstructing certain preconceptions that myself and wider society hold and using my survey results to test my subsequent theories.

Literature Review

For this research project, I have divided my literature review in two. Firstly there is the question of what academic texts I have consulted and their degree of validity. Secondly I will review a selection of varying literature that has dealt with Queer as folk and the issues it raises, all the time looking from a Communication Studies angle.

Two useful academic texts I have used are *A Handbook of Qualitative Methodologies for Mass Communication Research* by Bruhan Jensen, K & Jankowsi, N.W (1991) and *Researching Communications* by Deacon, D, Pickering M, Golding, P & Murdock, G (1999).

Both have proved useful. I found Jensen & Jankowsi to have a more theoretical approach with detailed insights into how many Communication methodologies and techniques came into practice, such as Semiotics. Relating these concepts to working theories in the field I found Sonia Livingstone's Making *Sense of Television* detailed discourse of semiotic analysis of soaps as a framework against which I could position my analysis of QAF. However in the area I am studying, a visual text (television programme) I found there to be a discourse concerned at the lack of communication progress in this area. For example *Researching Communications* explains:

When we turn to images, however, we have much less to go on since work on the visual dimensions of media remains relatively under developed [Deacon, Pickering, Golding & Murdock 1999:185]

Since Jensen & Jankowsi published in 1991, analysis in this area was even less developed than it is today, so while I have attempted to take on board some of the issues raised, I found myself concentrating on the other text.

I found *Researching Communications* to be valuable for several reasons. Firstly while it deals with the theory, it is written from a practical viewpoint so it has been a valuable guide to correctly utilising the relevant methodologies. It is a joint effort from four lecturers and professors increasing the scope of what the text covers. Its recent publication date means some of the more recent Communication discourses, especially advancement in analysing images, are covered in greater depth.

Obviously not all literature I consulted would prove to be useful, I consulted the Sexuality and Culture online journal[3] but found it to be largely American-centric and the detailed case-studies failed to largely deal with gay representation on TV.

Regarding the literature produced following the show, there has been little academic study into the shows' effects due to its recent airing. However the show has the potential to affect things that would not normally appear obvious. For example the 14th May edition of the Metro newspaper (a free paper for Londoners) reviewed a restaurant opening in Soho, Manto, that had gained popularity due to the original Manto appearing in the Manchester based series. As an attempt to reach across traditional boundaries, mimicking the show, the restaurant aimed to have a sexually ambivalent atmosphere, catering for both heterosexuals and homosexuals.

In more immediate circles Queer as Folk has been written about fairly extensively. Academically Billingham has a specific chapter on the show (see section on Content and Textual analysis). The writer of the show, Russell T Davies has made prolific comments on the series, with some interesting information revealed on both the released CDs by dance specialists Almighty to include and supplement both UK series' modern soundtracks. A prolific writer, on the first he details how in TV in the past there had often been gay characters but never ones centre stage. Popular shows attempt to reach as wide an audience as possible, so the temptation to target a particular minority exclusively is obviously a narrow bridge to walk. Dated February 1999, Davies writes

---

[3] www.csulb.edu/~asc/journal.html

And striving to make it good drama - never mind that it's gay, never mind the issues, they [Channel 4] just wanted it to be good   [QAF Album: 1999]

As a note of context here it needs to be considered who commissioned the show. Channel 4 came in to being in the 1980's as an alternative to the mainstream BBC and ITV. I found an interesting resource here to be A Queer Romance by Paul Burston and Colin Richardson as they describe Channel 4's initial struggles to gain a distinctive identity aside from the mainstream.

In particularly how *Outrage* heading by the direct activist Peter Tatchell launched a petition for a gay representation on TV with a call for a gay program to 'sit' with a black program and similar minorities. A major part of its brief was towards minority programming, as an alternative the Channel quickly gained a reputation for courting controversy (A similar discourse can be seen today with C5's reputation for showing soft pornographic movies). So the channel may seem bold in retrospect but it was only fulfilling its brief in a similar way to ITV commissioning a Sunday drama series for example. Channel 4 was deemed the natural home for the series according to Davies (see Appendix 1) because of its remit, though of course there was the risk that the show's content would have a negative impact. Surprisingly Davies makes the point that the then, commissioning editor for ITV, David Liddiment said he would have picked up the show, though tellingly from a commercial channel, this was told in retrospect when all the publicity and high video, CD and DVD sales was apparent.

From the QAF 2 album dated February 2000, to coincide when the sequel series aired; Davies commented

Let's be honest. When you're commissioned to write a late night drama for Channel 4 you expect viewing figures to match the guest-list for a teetotal prayer meeting.   [QAF 2 album: 2000]

In reality the Show's performance exceeded all expectations, regarding the programme's content, channel and time slot. It regularly achieved over 3.5 million viewers, being one of the few specialist minority programmes to cross over into the mainstream, with a demographic of heterosexual women and their partners being a considerable boost. I will examine the communication reasons for this success, in my report sections on analysis of my results and analysis of a section of the show.

As research into society's homophobia and the series, the 5th May 2000 edition of The Pink Paper had an interesting article by Michael Osborn where the ITC revealed their latest TV complaints (These can be obtained through their website www.itc.org.uk). The article reports there had been thirteen for Queer as Folk 2 but twelve were regarding a poor taste joke about the late Jill Dando and not homosexuality. This is in contrast to the thirty complaints received for the original series. The head of ITC makes the point:

The gay issue is more discussed by people now and the more this continues the less prejudice there will be   [Osborn M 2000:32]

A powerful riposte to those who looked towards the show's first episode with its provocatively controversial gay sex and labelled the entire series as shock material and no more, in particular tabloid TV critics. Of particular note here was the Daily Mails reaction which saw the show as diametrically opposed to its courtship of conservative middle England sensibilities. I take the stance that had there not been an uproar caused and the provocation of subsequent discussion then how will prejudices ever be broken down?

In the February 2000 edition of Gay Times, in an interview with Russell T Davies, there is the irony of the communications media battling against itself. In a commodity driven market this can have a restraining effect on right wing opinion, for example Davies here observes that Gary Bushell in his regular showbiz column for *The Sun* newspaper originally said after the airing of the first episode:

Boycott all the companies who advertise in the commercial breaks of this programme [Marr D 2000:38]

This was to spectacularly backfire as Rupert Murdock, having joint ownership of the paper and the dominant satellite TV provider; Sky which was advertising in QAF commercial breaks. Consequently Bushnells objections to the show were quickly stifled by episode five.

The May 2000 edition of Fluid magazine has an interesting article that sheds some light on the contrast between Queer and Folk and contemporary TV. Paul Clements examines the fact that gays in soap operas such as Eastenders are consistently shown as banal and so Queer as Folk's opposite approach making 'Manchester look like LA' while extravagant, could go some way to why the new portrayal caused such controversy.

Method

In order to pilot study my research question effectively, I needed to consider the different methodologies available to me.

The first question I asked myself was the balance my research would take between qualitative and quantitative research. I have used a balance of both, some qualitative elements, drawing on my own experience and research in the field and then quantitative techniques to reinforce, such as my surveys.

Bearing in mind I am dealing with an ever more visible minority group I wanted to design a survey with a flexible structure to allow maximum feedback. I needed to consider the individual advantages and disadvantages each methodology would carry.

Regarding the method of surveys, although ultimately I would have liked a universal level of representation, within the limited scope of this research I decided it necessary to target specifically to maximise the utility of my responses. I realise this biases my findings, as gay people were not the only audience to have watched the series.   However I believe this is acceptable considering there was an original target audience.   Therefore to achieve theoretical sampling I took my surveys to BLAG; (Bisexual Lesbian Gay Group) based in Southend on Sea. It is an institution designed to offer mutual support. Secondly I utilised the electronic media and sent my questionnaire via e-mail to friends who had watched the show.   The construction of the survey would obviously determine my research, so I found reference to *The art of Asking Questions* published in 1951 by S.L.Payne useful. She identifies four factors that affect responses to questions, which I have attempted to consider during the drafting of my survey but will reflect upon when I analyse my results.   Firstly behaviour, that is where people may simply lie.   Beliefs that may override a more social response. Attitudes, where they answer in a way they would like the situation to be and attributes where they answer in a way they believe the questioner would find appropriate. I have viewed the different strands within a particular methodology as open to interpretation and so my self-completion questionnaire, while it is obviously structured, also allows for some more qualitative answers via open questions.

I chose Surveys in order that I could acquire a large amount of information which I could then statistically analyse. Comparisons from different respondents can be examined and through targeting I can be representative of the primary group. However I am aware of the disadvantages this method entails which I have attempted to minimise. Primarily I will be influencing the responses by my choice of questioning and there is a limit to their responses, a factor less prevalent in face to face or phone interviews as those communication methods provoke dialogism.

As an element of my survey and research is social investigation, the interviewee's spontaneity is reduced, as they have to think of appropriate responses. There are the more technical constraints of different interpretation of the questions and inaccurate answering. However as I researched my method previous to implementation I feel my analysis will explain how I tried to overcome these disadvantages.

Drawing from *Researching Communications*, the point is made:

It is in qualitative research that the automatic assumption that 'big is beautiful' is most directly challenged   [Deacon, Pickering , Golding & Murdock 1999:43]

As I am researching into a delicate human topic I could afford to keep my sample modest and my total is 20 (see Appendix 2). While I realise this is deemed inadequate in social science terms, I feel certain advantages justify me in this approach. Firstly at this size the usual problem of non-response could be kept under control as I was present with half of the survey respondents and could answer any queries they had. Likewise e-mail affords a similar quality though non-response to certain questions is inevitable. Secondly there is the difficulty in obtaining useful results on a specific matter concerning sexuality, as my questionnaire largely relied on respondents having seen the show therefore a widespread general sample would have brought little benefit. By targeting in this way I feel I have attained a good cross-section, namely individuals I know through association of both sexuality's, a local gay youth group and a global perspective via French and Canadian OAF sites. (www.queerasfolk.fr.st and www.queerasfolk.ca respectively) From communication with these sites individuals requested questionnaires via e-mail. Thirdly the validity of the size of my sample is substantially complemented by an exclusive telephone interview with the series creator Russell T Davies as this gives an authoritative comparison for my results (see Interview section and Appendix 1). These ethnographic approaches have considerable advantages as established by David Morley's *The Nationwide Audience* (1980) as they allow me to discuss media consumption in an everyday context while interpreting individuals responses from differing social backgrounds (see Results section).

I would say my research has a degree of stratified random sampling as qualified by Jensen & Jankowsi, in so far as I selected subjects that shared similar characteristics.

Namely their sexuality, but was selective above simple random selection because I was aware of the need to be representative within the sample so age and gender were (secondary) considerations. The main thrust of my sampling though is undoubtedly theoretical because I reasoned this would be the group who would give the most validity to my personal theories. Going to BLAG presented me with the chance of strong convenience sampling where I hoped that the social group present would present a cluster of particularly interesting opportunities to research. I also felt this elevated the method above a basic self-completion questionnaire because the environment allowed for some discussion. My presence also removed the demoralising factor of a distant questioner and respondent. This has been beneficial to the extent to which my open questions have been answered. Accordingly the response to my open questions was also excellent from the questionnaires I received from www.queerasfolk.ca as they share specific interest in the area.

I quickly realised that simple closed questions revealing yes and no answers would be of little evaluative gain to my research question as Deacon et al comments:

Organic and responsive approach is essential to generate deeper insights into subtle and complex perceptions and beliefs. [Deacon, Pickering, Golding & Murdock 1999:63]

Bearing the above factors in mind, I knew to keep the questionnaire short to maintain interest. Secondly to start with simple open questions to lead the candidate in. I wanted my questions to provoke thought much as the show I am researching did so I included an ambiguous question; 'Do you think Queer as Folk represents normal gay life?' with a follow up question purely designed to record their thoughts.

Initially I piloted my study to ten of my colleagues to gain feedback for revision. While I gained interesting quantifiable results, this revealed the need for more open questions as these would give me more revealing answers with the possibility to identify if any common broad themes emerged (see Results section). With this progression I introduced questions of increasing complexity, my questions 12, 13, & 14 are double questions. On the second review this appeared sustainable because the questions were dealing with subject matter that would be very familiar to the respondents and which referred to an earlier more closed question. I have taken further liberties with the method such as asking emotive questions Like 'Have you experienced homophobia'
because I have not had the concern of producing a generalised survey though that would be a consideration if I was to further this research in the future.

Results

For my results refer to my included questionnaires (Appendix 2). The main results from the quantitative question are below:

Quantitative Question Responses		Totals
1 Age	14-18	3
	19-24	8
	25-30	3
	30-40	2
	40+	4
2 Sex	Male	14
	Female	6
3 Did you watch the fist series of QAF?	Yes	18
	No	2
4 How did you find out about the series?	TV Advert	12
	Print Ad	6
	Billboard	2
	Radio	
5 Did you watch the second series of QAF?	Yes	14
	No	6
6 Does QAF represent 'normal' gay life?	Yes	11
	No	10
8 Reasons for watching QAF 2?	Reputation	
	Drama	6
	Acting	2
	Homosexuality	10
	Sex	
	Drugs	
	Humour	
9 Have you experienced Homophobia?	School	13
	Home	6
	Work	9
	Leisure	12
10 QAF assists liberalising society?	Yes	9
	No	2
	Undecided	8
15 Why the controversy?	Never been done	14
	Purely to shock	5
	Political	4
16 Do gay people get enough representation on TV?	Yes	3
	No	17

These raise some interesting points, regarding questions 1 and 2 these reinforce the notion of the programme achieving wide appeal as there is a wide age demographic while emphasising the appeal to 19-24 years olds with a degree of sex pre-occupation that the show established in the first episode.

There is also a surprisingly high female respondent considering there was only minority female representation on the show[4]. Question 4 highlights the TV as the dominant medium for such a show which coincides with Davies opinion of the irrelevance of print media (see Appendix 1 and Interview section). With question 6 the sample is roughly split in half which is inevitable, as it is impossible to achieve universal representation. Question 8 reveals the fact that despite the show being applauded for quality of drama, acting and humour[5], homosexuality was the main reason for watching the show implying a lack of representation currently in the media which ties in with the response to question 16. Question 9 reveals some of the reasons for the show's success by striking a chord with sensitive issues, for example school was seen as the area of most homophobia that was tackled by the shows' inclusion of a schoolboy (Nathan Maloney) at a time when section 28 was under review. Lastly regarding questions 10 and 15 such scenes that had never been seen before on British television were seen as the main factor behind the controversy generated with opinion split over whether this led to healthy debate (lowering the age of consent) or draw unwanted attention to vulnerable minorities. Homophobia, despite the perceived liberalisation of society that institutions such as the ITC appear to believe in (as mentioned previously), it is still of real concern.

For question 11 I have displayed the results in a graph (see Appendix 3). My sample preference was clearly for QAF and its uncompressing portrayal of homosexuality. Equally this highlighted the banality of current shows, with soaps coming a consistent last. However the question is biased in so far as some of the sample (French and Canadian respondents) did not have equal access to all the shows as their UK counterparts had.

Moving onto analysing my qualitative question results I have identified the following broad trends:

---

[4] See Appendix 1 for Davies' remarks on how he was accused of being unrepresentative of lesbians, even though he did not set out with universal representation in mind
[5] The main character of QAF, Stuart Alan Jones played by Aiden Gillian was voted as the 41st best TV character ever by an online poll conducted by Channel 4 for their 100 Best Television characters Ever programme (6/05/01)

7) <u>What things (in QAF) do you think should have been covered?</u>

The female respondents, mostly 30 and above wanted to see more portrayal of everyday life outside of Babylon & Canal street which were the central clubbing locations of the series. Only two males followed this line. As apparent justification for Davies not to intend to make the show issue based, only one male wanted to see AIDS/safer sex addressed. I would argue this is because of viewer fatigue with previous shows pre-occupation with such issues (for example the long running HIV storyline in Eastenders).

12) <u>Which of the said shows would you most like to see return and why?</u>

6 out of 10 answering wanted QAF for various reasons; interestingly one 14-18 respondent said it helped with him coming out.[6] One female respondent wanted Eastenders, making the point that as a hugely popular show it could be used for positive influences.

14) <u>Which QAF character did you most identify with and why?</u>

Vince Tyler was most popular wit 2 females and 5 males because they could identify with his genuine intentions and disastrous love life! While Nathan Mahoney proved popular with the younger respondents who were of a similar age to the character, thus serving as a positive role model. Therefore a strong degree of character association was evident, undoubtedly a significant reason behind the shows success.

17) <u>What are your current 3 favourite programmes?</u>

A large variety of shows displayed that while gay programming was popular viewers were certainly not ghettoised in their choices, with older respondents favouring universal news, current affairs and gritty drama.

---

[6] "Being gay has never been so cool!" Heat magazine November 1999

Interview

Following on from my analysis of the questionnaire results, please refer to my interview with the series creator; Russell T Davies (Appendix 1) that was arranged initially with the co-operation of Red Productions, the Manchester based production company responsible for the series.

I had pre-selected areas of relevance brought up from my own reading and the questionnaire results and had give these topic areas in advance to Davies so as he was able to prepare answers. I feel the following points are of particular relevance to my study.

As example of society's persistent homophobia, *Becks* the German beer company that were sponsoring a range of C4's shows withdrew their sponsorship after the only the second episode because of a feared negative impact.

Regarding my questioning of the banality of current programming Davies concurs that the shows production values were excellent and his notion of hitting the market at the right time co-insides with the delicate political climate I described in the introduction.

The notion of gay backlash is particularly interesting, as Billingham describes Queer as Folk as a Hetrotpia, where heterosexuality is marginalized. This was clearly a notion that many found uncomfortable, against an upbringing of conventional socialisation. Indeed in Channel 4's *Right to Reply* programme after the first episode had aired, featured Anglia Mason, head of equality group, Stonewall and a gay 'Joe public' strongly criticising the shows aberrant morality.

Davies raises the notion of globalisation as the show; originally thought to graphic for American viewers has now been successfully adapted to the US market (as well as a considerable global fan-base as the various countries' fan-sites demonstrates). On seeing the first three episodes[7] of the USA adaptation I could see how the show, while retaining the graphic depictions of sex had been adapted to American sensibilities. Issues around Religion were raised that were not present in the UK original as well as an amplification of consumerism and capitalism by raising the equivalent character of Nathan, (in the UK version, a working class background) to having a privileged lifestyle and going to a private school.

---

[7] 2001 Gay and Lesbian Film Festival at the National Film Festival, London 28/03/01 – 11/04/01

14

Content & Textual Analysis

Analysing the opening three minutes of the show revealed reasons for the controversy and unconformity within this drama.

There were immediately close-ups of the three (as yet) unknown main characters, talking to the camera (viewer) instead of the usual gradual association. The attractiveness was increased by strong use of primary colour.

There was an unusual amount of music variation, changing 7 times and helping to link the meeting of two characters that would form the framework for the series. The camera work is very fast and utilising numerous techniques. The last distinguishing feature is when a 15-year-old asks an innocent question, only to be hurled a flurry of expletives. However beyond such quantitative considerations Billingham expertly utilises textual analysis as a way to interpret produced meaning, particularly regarding the three main characters. Unfortunately such detailed analysis it excessive to the scope of this project as I have already determined the broad trends that differentiate this particular drama.

Conclusion

Obviously I faced difficulties in this assignment, ranging from difficulties in arranging interviews, to size of samples, to difficulty in printing off old correspondence! But I have found the project a challenging and rewarding experience considering the time restraints imposed. In reflection, the challenge with this project has been proving that public perception has changed and that my assignment touches on numerous areas outside of my scope. However aside from the predictable right wing (print) media I would say it is a sign of progress that there was not more controversy stirred. One of the most important features that I feel set the program apart was that it examined the sex lives of gay men; something that had been rather coyly sidelined in previous dramatic television treatments of homosexuality in Eastenders et al. I would say within the confines of this project, that the controversy was such precisely because there were more factors at play than is normal. That the banality of current TV dealing with gay related issues (not TV as a whole because my study revealed a wide preference of programmes, many not gay related at all) set up a standard waiting to be beaten. The question of society's homophobia is obviously harder to distinguish, and there was an element of outrage from a prejudiced viewpoint that such issues should not be discussed on TV but if the institutions that regulate society are setting an example, then society is bound to follow in the future.[©]

[©] Ryan Edwards 2001

16

Bibliography

Deacon D, Pickering M, Golding P & Murdock G (1999) *Researching Communications* London: Arnold

Bruhan Jensen, K & Jankowsi, N.W (1991) *A Handbook of Qualitative Methodologies for Mass Communication Research*

Billingham P (2000) *Sensing the City through Television* Intellect

Burston P, Richardson C *A Queer Romance* (1995) Chapter 11

Livingstone S *Making Sense of Television* 3rd edition (1998)

Russell T Davies, *Queer as Folk* CD sleeve (February 1999) Almighty Records

Russell T Davies, *Queer as Folk 2* CD sleeve (February 2000) Almighty Records

Osborn M, *No Cause for Complaint* Pink Paper article (5th May 2000)

Marr D, *Spunk on the Screen* Gay times article February 2000

Fluid Magazine May 2000 p.66-73

References

Payne S, L *The art of Asking Questions* (1951) Princeton University Press

Nightingale V *Studying Audiences The Shock of the Real* (1996)

Docherty D, Morrison D, E Tracey, M *Keeping faith? Channel Four and its audience* (1998)

Creekmur C, K & Doty A *Out in Culture* (1995)

Claire A, *Masculinity In Crisis* (2000)

Tee, J www.queerasfolk.ca (2001)

Renault, S www.queerasfolk.fr.st (2001)

www.csulb.edu/~asc/journal.html (2001)

www.itc.org.uk (2001)

Heat magazine November 1999

Right to Reply (06/11/99) Channel 4

Appendix 1 Russell T Davies, writer of Queer as Folk Interview

Sponsorship

Becks were sponsoring C4 drama as a whole - not just QAF. They never read our scripts; they had no contact with us. But when they pulled out, there was never any danger of us being pulled off their air.

Manchester

No choice. I live in Manchester. The producer lives in Manchester. Red was set up to produce stuff in Manchester. So there was no debate.

Audience

3 - 4 million was not that massive, but it was good for C4. There was a massive publicity campaign. And it was a fantastic piece of telly. It looked good; the music was good. We hit the right climate at the right time.

Pitched at C4?

We talk to broadcasters and editors all the time about what they want. The first conversation I had about QAF were with C4. David Liddiment said afterwards that he would have screened it, but that was in retrospect.

Did you expect more critical backlash?

I expect a greater savaging, but we were largely ignored by the tabloids. In any case, all those acre of newsprint are irrelevant. Editorials still read as though it were 1910. The viewing figures rose largely through word of mouth.

Gay backlash

I expected that. There is ghetto thinking. People make up their minds before they've even seen the show. QAF drew attention to the sex lives of gay men. In Britain, sex fascinates and frightens people at the same time.

Has QAF opened doors to other gay programming, like Metrosexuality

Maybe, but that man had been trying to get that show on the air for years. Naked Civil Servant went out at 9pm on ITV, but it didn't change the face of TV. NCS and QAF were just blips. But things are getting better, though slowly.

Representation.

I gave a talk recently at which a mad woman asked why TV didn't deal with lesbianism more. These people don't even watch TV. I took her through the list of lesbian characters on TV at the moment.

Spin off show on C4.

I don't know why it didn't go out. I merely had a 3-line letter saying No thank you.

US version.

I had very little input. There were friendly chats. I wen out these, but it was a publicity thing really.

Disagreements with US?

I didn't like the names, but that is a tiny thing. The funniest thing was that they made Jason very rich only because he was wearing a school uniform. They thought he was going to a boarding school, not a state school.

In US but not UK version:

Character went into a straight club. We just thought it was very funny. It wasn't supposed to be a ground breaking moment.

Appendix 2 Queer As Folk Questionnaire

1. Age
      14-18   19-24   25-30   30-40   40+

2. Sex
      Male   Female

3. Did you watch the first series of Queer As Folk?
      Yes   No

4. So how did you get to know about the programme and/or its sequel?
      Television Advert
      Print Advert
      Radio
      Friends
      Billboard

5. Did you watch the second series of Queer as Folk?
      Yes   No

6. Do you think Queer as Folk represents 'normal' gay life?
      Yes   No

7. If no, what things do you think should have been covered?

8. What was your main reason for watching Queer as Folk 2?
      Drama
      Acting
      Homosexuality
      Sex
      Drugs
      Humour
      Reputation

9. Have you experienced homophobia?
      At school
      At home
      At work
      At leisure

10. Do you think programmes such as Queer as Folk help to create a more liberal society?
      Yes   No   Undecided

11. The following programmes have all tackled gay issues, place them in order of preference (1 being your favourite)

> Queer as Folk
> Queer as folk 2
> Gaytime TV
> This Life
> Eastenders
> Brookside
> Metrosexuality

12. Which of the above shows would you most like to see return and why?

13. Which of the above shows would you least like to see return and why?

14. Which Queer as Folk character did you most identify with and why?

15. Why do you think the opening episodes with underage gay sex and threesomes caused such controversy?
> Purely to shock
> Never been done before
> Political point

16. Do you think gay people get enough representation on TV?
> Yes   No

17. What are your current 3 favourite programmes:

Any other comments:

Thankyou for filling this in!

Appendix 3 Question 11 results graph

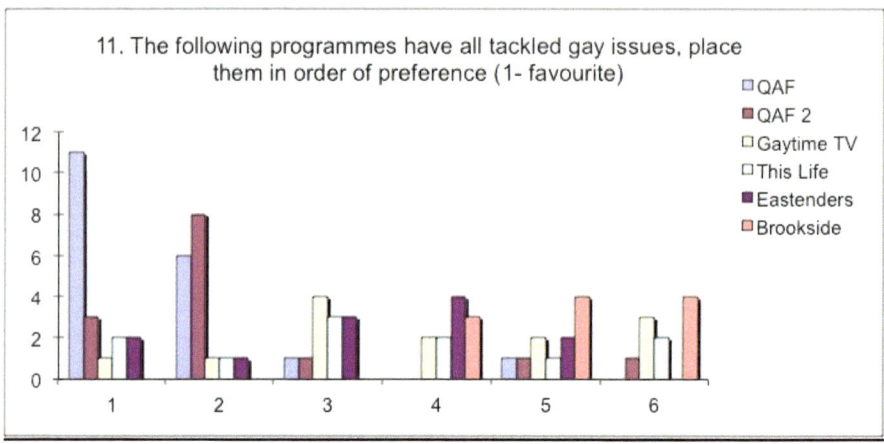

11. The following programmes have all tackled gay issues, place them in order of preference (1- favourite)

- ☐ QAF
- ■ QAF 2
- ☐ Gaytime TV
- ☐ This Life
- ■ Eastenders
- ☐ Brookside